For David & Lily
Beloved Parents & Grandparents

First BenBella Books Edition September 2004

BENBELLA

BenBella Books
6440 N. Central Expressway
Suite # 617
Dallas, TX 75206

Send feedback to feedback@benbellabooks.com
www.benbellabooks.com

Printed in Italy

Library of Congress Cataloging-in-Publication Data:

Kurzweil, Sonya.
Forever poems for now and then /
Sonya Kurzweil and Amy Kurzweil.
p. cm.
ISBN 1-932100-39-3
I. Kurzweil, Amy. II. Title.
PS3611.U735F67 2004
811'.6--dc22   2004007682

Cover design by Laksman Frank
Interior designed and composed by Laksman Frank

Distributed by Independent Publishers Group
To order call (800) 888-4741
www.ipgbook.com

Cover credits

top left Two Girls Reading, 1890-91
Pierre-Auguste Renoir, 1841-1919
French

top right The Starry Night, 1889
Vincent van Gogh, 1853-1890
Dutch

bottom left The Small Boy, 1938
Pablo Picasso, 1881-1973
Spanish

bottom right Woman with Cat, 1875
Pierre-Auguste Renoir, 1841-1919
French

back Girl with Tadpoles-Paloma, 1954
Pablo Picasso, 1881-1973
Spanish

End pages Credit

Day in The Life of a Little Girl, 1952
Norman Rockwell, 1911-1978
American

Forever Poems
for Now and Then

Sonya Kurzweil
and Amy Kurzweil

Contents

Two Girls Reading, 1890-91
Pierre-Auguste Renoir, 1841-1919
French

Friends

Some friends come and go
Now and then

Some friends come and stay
Some friends are forever

Even when they say goodbye
They are my favorite kind

Birthdays

I dream of birthdays
Especially mine
The friends
The food
The fun
And when the party's over
The gifts have just begun

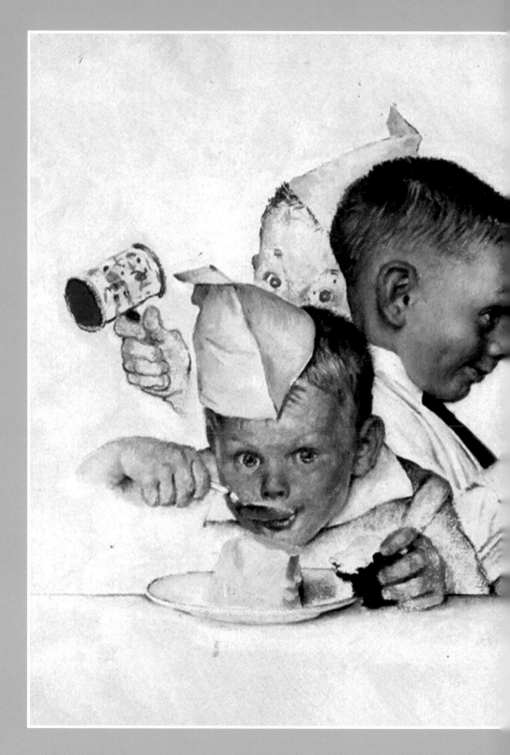

Day in the Life of a Little Girl, 1952
Norman Rockwell, 1911-1978
American

10

The Starry Night, 1889
Vincent van Gogh, 1853-1890
Dutch

Blue

Blue is beautiful
Blue is the sky
Blue are the bed sheets
Where I lie

Blue is the ocean
Where the waves roll in
Blue are my eyes
They twinkle, they spin

Campbell's Soup Cans, 1965
Andy Warhol, 1928-1987
American

Hungry

I want lunch
Give me food
If you don't
I might get rude

And I might just
Let you see
How bitterly bad
A boy can be

I think I'll have
Some carrots and peas
Some bread with jam
And crackers 'n' cheese
A pizza or two
With peppers and spice
And chocolate cake
And soup with rice
And bacon and eggs
And pretzels that snap

I know I can eat all that!

Leaves in Fall

Leaves blowing in the wind
Red, orange, brown
Squiggle helpless from the trees
Before floating down

These featherlike things
Perfect and small
Blend with smells of winter wood
As they fall

Trees stand tall and proud
Watch leaves on the ground
Colorful seasonal leaves
Abound

At the Edge of Fontainebleau, 1885
Alfred Sisley, 1839-1899
French

Halloween

Halloween is out of sight
Sure to give an awful fright
In the deep dark dead of night

Halloween has candy and more
Gypsies, ghosts, goblins galore
Could be lurking behind the door

Spooky shadows on the stair
Creeping near they seem to stare
Bulging eyeballs here and there

Halloween, detail, 1955
Grandma Moses, 1860-1961
American

Winter Ice

Winter weather is so nice
When the lake is full of ice
With skates in hand I'm out the door
Hoping for lots of time before
The ice melts

A Winter Landscape, detail of skaters, 1565
Pieter Brueghel the Elder, 1525/30-1569
Flemish

The Race

I hop on my sled
My brother does too
"I'll race you" he calls
So that's what we do

Past the post
Past the tree
Flying fast
He zooms by me

And then he looks back
Which he shouldn've done
He falls off his sled
It looks like I've won!

Snow in his hair
And a grin on his face
He laughs as he says
"Guess you won the race"

But, I wondered...
About that grin...
Did he...
Let me win?

Sledding In Central Park, 1998
Robert Caulfeild, 1930-
American

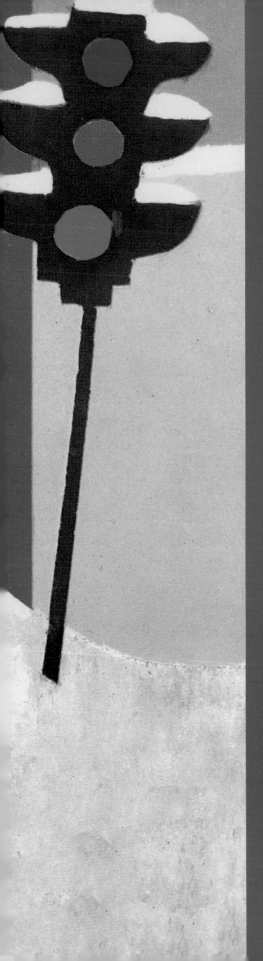

Footprints in Snow

I love to make footprints in snow
Patterns from A to Z
The snow goes squish or it goes squash
Whatever the case may be

I jump and pat or I go splat
For all the world to see
I crunch and slide or I glide
Ever so gracefully

But now and then with a grin
I slip sloppily
Hoping to land in winter's puff
Soft and feathery

The Snowy Day, book cover, 1962
Ezra Jack Keats, 1916-1983
American

Seeing Snow

In my wonderland of white
Blankets cover grounds
Hugging them tight
Trees sport gowns of silk and lace
As birds tweet with delight

In this seasonal fashion show
The fabric of choice is silky snow

I wish to join this white parade
Knowing that the scene is made
For trees and leaves
And birds of pearl
And one curious little girl

The Magpie, detail, 1869
Claude Monet, 1840-1926
French

New Spring Leaves

Spring leaves
Freshly grown
Freshly green

Reborn with the season
Newly sprouted buds
Bigger each day

With rain
In time, in space
They find their grace

Filling in emptiness
With dewey tenderness

Spring, 1878
Alfred Stevens, 1823-1906
Belgian

29

Summer

Summer summer
Swimming and bikes
These are things
I really likes

Matin d'été, detail, 2001
Michel Delacroix, 1933-
French

To the Beach, 1995
Ray Ellis, 1921-
American

Les Deux Amis, 1994
Michel Delacroix, 1933-
French

31

Summer Rainy Day

View goes gray
On a summer rainy day

Yellow slicker and cap roll by
On a bike in the distant sky
Birds fly in the quiet drizzle

It's a day for poets and readers
For bathing leaves
For growing flowers
For replenishing ponds
For remembering psalms

For watching the fog lift
Revealing islands far
For watching the sky clear
And a new day appear

Fog, 1874
Alfred Sisley, 1839-1899
French

Water Lily

Water Lily you're so silly
When I pat you on the belly
Wobble and bounce
Each time I pounce
And sometimes you quiver
Shimmering water on your leaves

Water Lilies, detail, 1905
Claude Monet, 1840-1926
French

Late in summer flowers almost done
I search and see an occasional one
Pearly white, quiet and still
I slip into your leafy house paddling
Softly around your vines

Surprise dunk!
Under you go
Back and forth
To and fro, but
Quickly gaining
Your repose

Elusive Dancers

In the flowers
In the trees
Weaving in
And out with ease

Chase em left
Chase em right
Chase em day
Chase em night

Watch em flutter
Watch em fly
Watch em dance
In the sky

The Small Boy, 1938
Pablo Picasso, 1881-1973
Spanish

Butterfly Kisses

Butterfly kisses
Full of wishes
So delicious

So delicious
Full of wishes
Butterfly kisses

Butterfly kisses
So delicious
Full of wishes

Full of wishes
So delicious
Butterfly kisses

Full of wishes
Butterfly kisses
So delicious

So delicious
Butterfly kisses
Full of wishes

Moonlit Landscape, 1874
Jean-Baptiste-Camille Corot, 1796-1875
French

Shimmering Moon

Shimmering moon
On crystal lake
Are you real or
Are you fake?

Are you a spotlight
On the shore?
Making me wish
For something more?

Dancing light
You make me dream
Of a more
Romantic scene

Woman with Cat, 1875
Pierre-Auguste Renoir, 1841-1919
French

And More Fluff

And he's always there
    for me
    at night
    with warm fluff
    on my bed
And brown
And black
And white
    with no tail
    just a stump
And furry legs
    with paws in snow
And snow on his nose
And tracks on my bed
And more fluff
And more fluff
And more fluff
And more. . . .

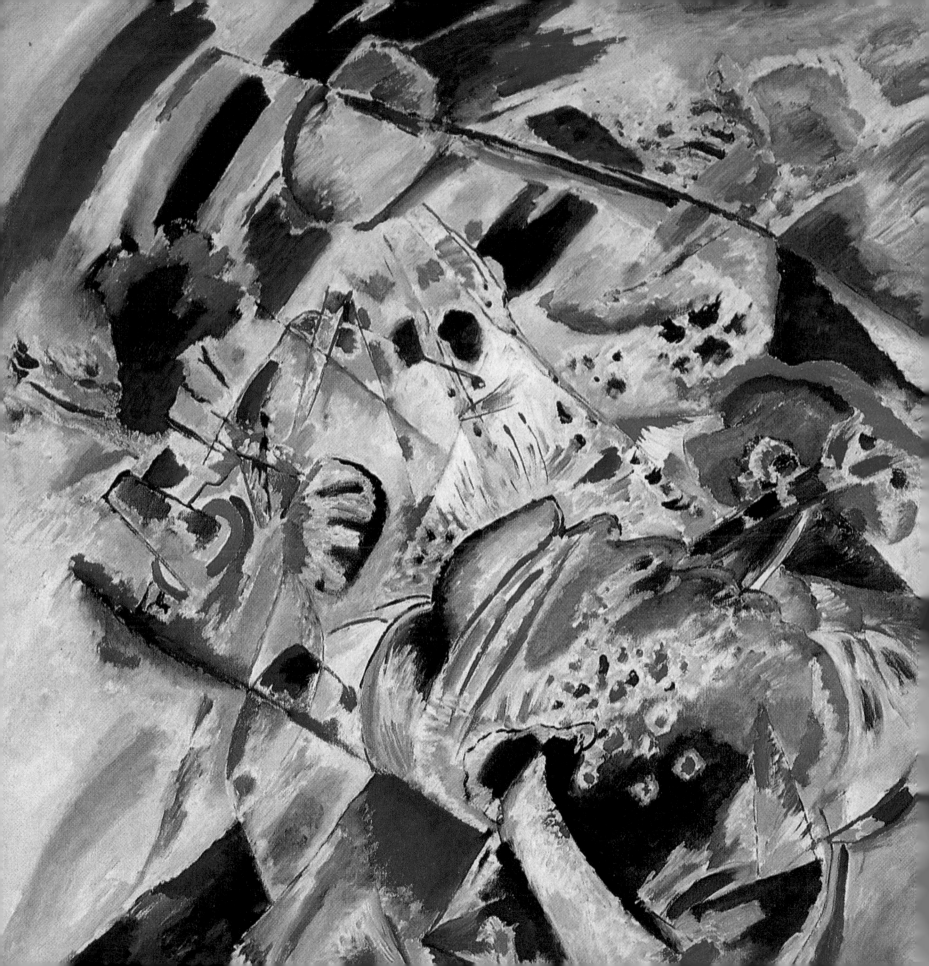

Messy Room

Ripped up papers
My room is a mess
Buttons are lost
And the dolls aren't dressed

Often when I turn around
I discover on the ground
Something lost
That now is found

I trip on something
Not knowing just what
And over I go
Onto my butt

Not sure just what's
Been broken
I look up and see
The door open

It's Mom
Finding me stuck
She rolls her eyes
And helps me pick up

Morning Poem

Open eyes
Lift head
Get your bottom
Out of bed

Three Ages of Women, detail, 1905
Gustav Klimt, 1862-1918
German

46

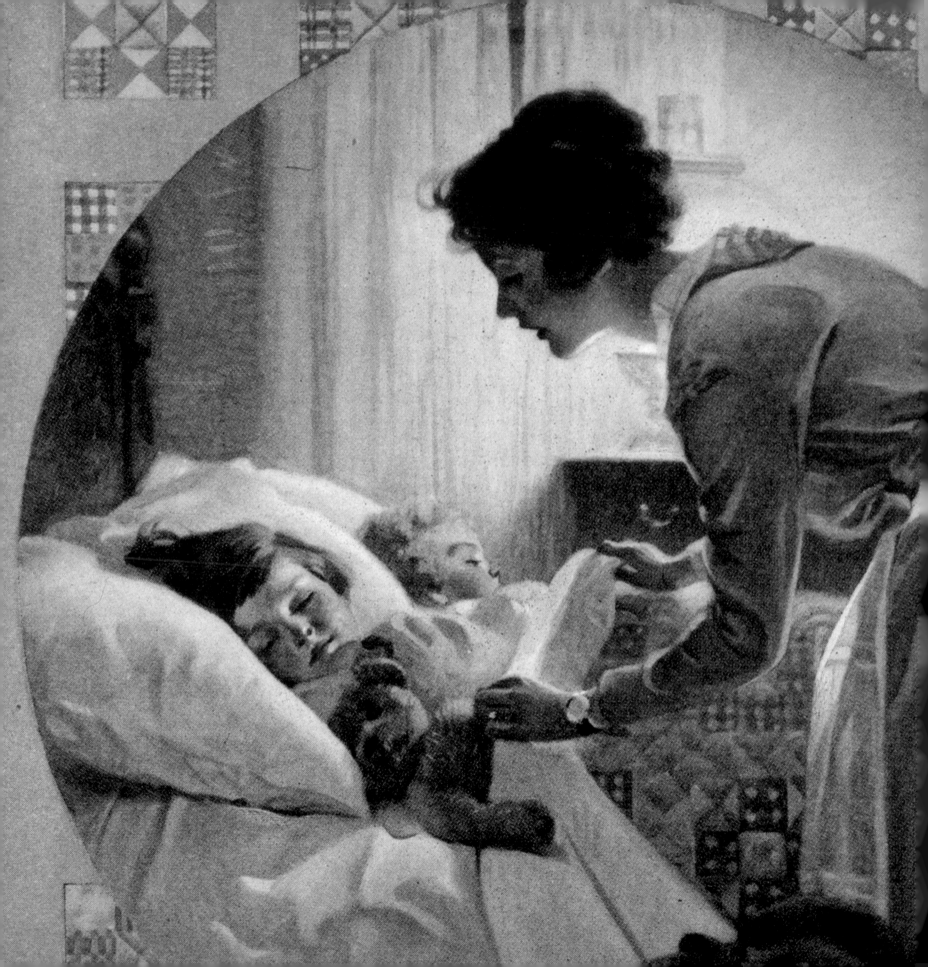

Evening Poem

Close eyes
Breathe deep
Very soon
You'll be asleep

Mother Tucking Children into Bed, detail, 1921
Norman Rockwell, 1894-1978
American

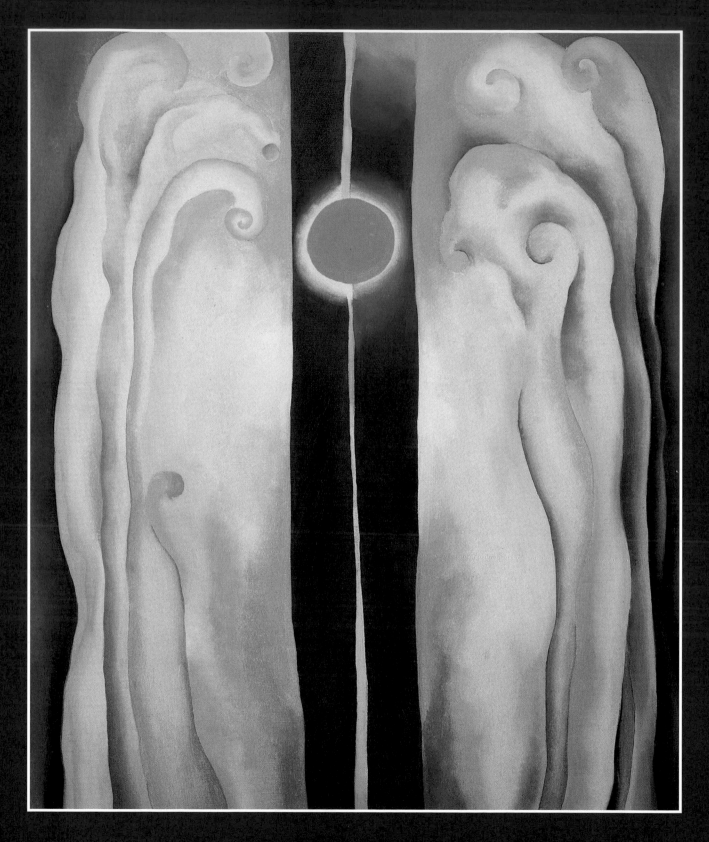

Pink Moon and Blue Lines, 1923
Georgia O'Keefe, 1887-1986
American

Setting Sun

Setting Sun
Each day a different one

Sometimes with streaks of pink and blue
Sometimes with none

One day light ribbons through clouds
Other days are solid blues and grays

After the blaze, darkening haze
Shapes unspun, formless sum

Day is done

Glossary of Art Movements
Included in the Book

Abstract Art

A type of Modern Art that creates vivid designs with lines, shapes and colors that have little direct connection to physical things found in reality. The artist expresses himself purely through the use of form and color. It is also referred to as "nonrepresentational art" because it sometimes does not appear to represent specific objects or scenes, but expresses abstractions, such as feelings or actions. (Kandinsky)

Folk Art

Pictures of scenes with many details of daily life which seem to tell a story of a particular place and time. Folk artists were usually self-taught from rural or pre-industrial societies and are considered by art historians to be more closely related to craftsmen than fine artists. The term "folk" refers to the common people, often living in a village or rural area. (Delacroix)

Impressionism

A style of painting used mainly by French artists in the late 19th century. Impressionism combines many dabs or strokes of paint in unmixed colors to create pretty pictures of people, objects and nature scenes as they are found in real life. The build up of paint in impressionist paintings simulates light on the canvas to give the paintings a luminous quality. (Renoir)

Modern Art

A term commonly used to describe the style of art found in Europe and America in the 20th century. Various dates are used to mark the point at which modern art supposedly began. The most commonly chosen is 1863, the year that Manet first showed his painting, Le Déjeuner sur l'herbe (Picnic on the Grass) at the Salon de Refusés. However, the Modern Art movement was not a sudden new outlook on painting. It gradually developed over the course of a hundred years, reflecting new attitudes that placed special importance on exploring and experimenting particularly with forms, shapes and color. Modern Art includes abstract art, surrealism and pop art. (Chagall)

Pop Art

A movement of art which began mainly in America and Britain in the 1950's and 60's. Pop artists create interesting and colorful images with commonplace objects found in every day life (for example, road signs, soup cans, hamburgers) and with pictures of people from popular culture (for example, Marilyn Monroe and Mickey Mouse). The images are expressed in an exaggerated way as if to poke fun of the culture or lead the viewer to question the way she is living life. (Warhol)

Realism

A style of art which accurately depicts people, objects and scenes as they exist in real life and nature. Realism does not idealize or glorify subjects nor does it emphasize the artist's own personal feelings or feelings for his subjects. (Breugel)

Surrealism

A form of Modern Art, born at the end of World War 1, that brought the worlds of fantasy, dreams and the unconscious mind to the canvas. Surrealism is deeply rooted in the rich symbolism of literature. The surrealist painter seems to imagine a dreamlike place where logic is suspended and contradictions are allowed. (Dali)

Acknowledgements

Much credit for this little gem of a book goes to the designers Celia Black and Laksman Frank. Celia worked tirelessly to gain permissions from the far corners of the world for use of the artwork and could always be counted on for insightful perspectives. Laksman's design talents, competence and patience were a winning combination. Thanks to Irene Elios for designing the first rough draft of this book. Special thanks to Ray Kurzweil for his support, encouragement and help with editing. We could not have prevailed without his savoir faire.

Sonya Kurzweil and Amy Kurzweil
Newton, MA
March 12, 2004

Art Credits

Chagall, Marc.
Mother and Child and Centar 1957
© 2004 Artists Rights Society (ARS), New York / ADAGP, Paris.

Renoir, Pierre-Auguste.
Two Girls Reading circa 1890-1891
Oil on canvas, 22 5/16x19 in.
Los Angeles Country Museum of Art, Gift of Dr. and Mrs. Armand Hammer.
Photograph © 2003 Museum Associates / LACMA.

Rockwell, Norman.
Day in The Life of a Little Girl 1952
Oil on canvas, 45 x 42 in. Saturday Evening Post cover illustration of August 30, 1952
Collection of The Norman Rockwell Museum at Stockbridge, Massachusetts.

van Gogh, Vincent.
The Starry Night 1889
Oil on canvas, 29x36 ¼ in. Acquired through the Lillie P. Bliss Bequest. (472.1941)
The Museum of Modern Art, New York, NY Digital Image © The Museum of Modern Art / Licensed by SCALA / Art Resource, NY.

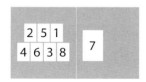

Warhol, Andy.
(#1) Campbell's Soup Can 1965.
Synthetic polymer paint and silkscreen ink on canvas, 36 x 24 in.
© Copyright the Andy Warhol Foundation, Inc. for the Visual arts / ARS, NY.
Photograph Credit: The Andy Warhol Foundation, Inc. / Art Resource, NY.

Warhol, Andy.
(#2) Campbell's Soup Can 1965
Synthetic polymer paint and silkscreen ink on canvas, 36 x 24 in.
© Copyright the Andy Warhol Foundation for the Visual Arts / ARS, NY.
Photograph Credit: The Andy Warhol Foundation, Inc. / Art Resource, NY.

Warhol, Andy.
(#3) Campbell's Soup Can 1965
Silkscreen ink on synthetic polymer paint on canvas, 36 1/8 x 23 in.
© Copyright the Andy Warhol Foundation for the Visual Arts / ARS, NY.
Photograph Credit: The Andy Warhol Foundation, Inc. / Art Resource, NY.

Warhol, Andy.
(#4) Campbell's Soup Can 1965
Synthetic polymer paint and silkscreen ink on canvas, 36 x 24 in.
© Copyright the Andy Warhol Foundation for the Visual Arts / ARS, NY.
Photograph Credit: The Andy Warhol Foundation, Inc. / Art Resource, NY.

Warhol, Andy.
(#5) Campbell's Soup Can 1965
Synthetic polymer paint and silkscreen ink on canvas, 36 ¼ x 24 ¼ in.
© Copyright the Andy Warhol Foundation for the Visual Arts / ARS, NY.
Photograph Credit: The Andy Warhol Foundation, Inc. / Art Resource, NY.
Menil Collection, Houston, Texas.

Warhol, Andy.
(#6) Campbell's Soup Can 1965
Synthetic polymer paint and silkscreen ink on canvas, 36 x 24 in.
© Copyright the Andy Warhol Foundation for the Visual Arts / ARS, NY.
Photograph Credit: The Andy Warhol Foundation, Inc. / Art Resource, NY.

Warhol, Andy.
(#7) Campbell's Soup Can 1965
Synthetic polymer paint and silkscreen ink on canvas, 36 x 24 in.
© Copyright the Andy Warhol Foundation for the Visual Arts / ARS, NY.
Photograph Credit: The Andy Warhol Foundation, Inc. / Art Resource, NY.

Warhol, Andy.
(#8) Campbell's Soup Can 1965
Synthetic polymer paint and silkscreen ink on canvas, 36 x 24 in.
© Copyright the Andy Warhol Foundation for the Visual Arts / ARS, NY.
Photograph Credit: The Andy Warhol Foundation, Inc. / Art Resource, NY.

Sisley, Alfred.
At the Edge of Fontainebleau 1885
Photo Credit: Pushkin Museum of Fine Arts, Moscow / Anatoly Sapronenkov / Superstock.

Grandma Moses.
Halloween 1955
© 1995 (renewed 1983) Grandma Moses Properties Co., New York.

Brueghel, Pieter the Elder.
Return of the Hunters 1565
(From the series six paintings of "the Seasons").
Kunsthistorisches Museum, Vienna
Photo Credit: Erich Lessing / Art Resource, NY.

Caulfield, Robert.
Sledding in Central Park 1998
Private Collection / Photo courtesy of The Caulfield Art Gallery, Woodstock, Vermont.

Keats, Ezra Jack.
The Snowy Day 1962
Cover illustration: Ezra Jack Keats, 1962
Puffin Books, NY, NY.

they fall

A pizza or two

With peppers and spice

es stand tall and proud

And chocolate cake

tch leaves on the ground

With gravy and rice

orful seasonal leaves

And bacon and eggs

ound

And pretzels that snap

I know I can eat all that!

Footprints in S

I love to make

Patterns from

The snow goes s

Whatever the ca

I jump and pa

For all the worl

I crunch and s

Ever so graceful

But now and t

I slip sloppily

Hoping to land

Soft and feathe

Friends

Some friends

Now and then

Some frie